G000091128

THE SPIRIT OF
EXMOOR RED DEER

RAY STONEMAN

HALSGROVE

First published in Great Britain in 2008

Copyright text and photographs © 2008 Ray Stoneman

British Library Cataloguing-in-Publication Data
A CIP record for this title is available from the British Library

ISBN 978 1 84114 710 9

HALSGROVE
Halsgrove House
Ryelands Industrial Estate
Bagley Road, Wellington
Somerset TA21 9PZ
Tel: 01823 653777
Fax: 01823 216796
email: sales@halsgrove.com
website: www.halsgrove.com

Printed and bound by D'Auria Industrie Grafiche Spa, Italy

Introduction

The red deer is Britain's largest land mammal and, with several thousand living on the open moor and using the woods and combes as places of safety, they are the most abundant deer on Exmoor.

A mature stag stands 125cm at the shoulder and weighs over 175kg, whereas hinds are about 20cm shorter and weigh not more than 100kg.

During the summer the coat is a rich dark red, whereas in the winter the thick coat is more brown or grey. Red deer moult twice a year in the spring and again in the autumn. With a mane from August to December, the neck of the stag is distinctly thicker than the neck of the hind.

Only the stags grow horns or antlers. These are cast and re-grown annually. Casting occurs in April and early May and the new growth is complete by August or September when the velvet, which protected the newly developing antler during the growth period, is shed. A good antler will have a strong main beam, and branching from it and nearest the head the brow point, a bey point in the middle and a trey point above. The top of the main beam divides into short points, and a seven year old stag should have brow, bey and trey points, and three short points at the top. This stag would be described on Exmoor as 'All his rights and three atop.' Between the ages of seven to ten a stag is in his prime, but at about twelve the antlers begin to 'go back' when the points atop tend to merge and flatten and the main beam becomes thinner. A healthy animal can live until it is about fifteen.

After a gestation period of around 34 weeks, calves are born in June and July and are usually dropped in moorland vegetation or by the edge of woodland. A single calf is normal and twins are rare.

Red deer eat a wide variety of food, including young shoots of heather, whortleberry, brambles, saplings and grass. They also feed on acorns, fungi, berries and ivy and can be a real pest to the farmer, raiding his fields for corn and root crops.

Their footprints are called 'slots' and may often be found in the mud near a stream where deer come to drink early in the morning or late in the evening. Stags and hinds both use wallows (wet muddy areas) in the summer months when the flies are prevalent, and the stags alone during the rutting season.

Their sight, hearing and sense of smell are excellent so it is quite difficult to get close to them. However, the summer is the best time to look for them on open moorland as the young grasses are at their most palatable. In winter they're more often seen on the fringes of farm-land while they may be found at any time in woodland.

WINTER

By the beginning of winter the red deer have generally settled into stag and hind herds with the calves and some prickets (young stags) remaining with the hinds. There are also some solitary stags which seek out some quiet corner for most of the year, generally lying up during the day before setting out to feed at dusk. Winter is the hardest time of the year for the deer with a general shortage of food and the now leafless woods offering little shelter from the winds. Heavy snow quickly buries most of their food but they continue to paw the ground for grass, whortleberry and heather, and search the woods for ivy and holly. Some will even descend to lower fields where grass and root crops may be more readily available.

**The monarch
of Exmoor**
A majestic red deer stag
near Wimbleball Lake.

You've been framed
The trees make a perfect frame for these hinds enjoying
the last rays of a crisp winter's day.

Opposite page:
All lads together
An impressive herd of stags at Southill on the edge of Exmoor.

Mist over Dulverton
A solitary hind takes an
early morning stroll.

Peek-a-boo
Making my way through the bracken at White Rocks,
near Hawkridge, I came face to face with this hind coming in the
opposite direction. I'm not sure who was the most surprised.

Opposite page:
Cold feet
The first snows of winter at Hawkridge, near Dulverton.

Frosty morning at Marsh Bridge
Judging by the size of his antlers, this young stag is about three years old.
A stag's antlers do not fully mature until the seventh year of life.

Up and over
Stags effortlessly jumping a fence at Southill in the evening sun.

Hind in a hurry
This picture shows the tremendous speed a hind can achieve.

Opposite page:
Hitching a ride
A young pricket stag with his short upright antlers.
Most likely in its second year of life.

A snowy gathering
A fine group of stags enjoying the winter sun at Southill.

SPRING

Spring brings warmer days and an abundance of food. Many hinds are now carrying calves which are due to be born in mid-summer and the stags are due to renew their antlers. The antlers are shed in April and early May. This is brought about by the drying up of the blood supply at the base of the antler until the connection with the pedicle becomes dead and brittle. Once the old antlers have been cast, the new ones start to develop and for the next three months they are covered by a thick skin known as velvet which protects the blood vessels and nerves. By early August the new growth will harden into solid bone and the velvet is rubbed off on a tree branch or shrub.

Old man of Exmoor
Spring moult.

Opposite page:
Time for a new coat

Young ladies of the Moor
Hinds – spring moult.

Lounging around
Stags resting in lush spring grass.

A cast antler found at Chilly Bridge, near Dulverton

Opposite page:
Lop sided
These stags have started to cast their antlers.

Look what I've found!

Can I help you?
A very pretty and inquisitive young stag.

Hinds in the early spring sunshine

Taking flight
This dramatic picture
shows just how high a
stag can actually jump.

Taking a bath

Setting sun
A group of stags in the early evening sun at Brendon Two Gates.

Sunset over Winsford Hill

SUMMER

June is the month when most red deer calves are born on Exmoor. The calf usually weighs between 15 and 20lbs. The first calf is born when the mother is two to four years old. For a few days, the new-born calf will lie quietly, well-camouflaged with its dappled russet coat blending in with the bracken. Eventually it is strong enough to run with its mother and join the herd. They stay together for at least a year. Towards the end of the summer the white spots on the youngsters fade away but up until their second birthday they can always be recognised by their smaller size.

Strictly come dancing
Hinds practicing their moves.

A lone stag in velvet

Nearly done
A herd of stags nearing the end of velvet.

Opposite page:
Shoo fly don't bother me
Numerous flies pester this
poor stag in velvet.

A calf suckling

Opposite page:
Bambi
A delightful red deer calf at White Rocks near Hawkridge.

Waiting for mum
Up and about but still camouflaged whilst waiting for its mother to return.

Growing up
This calf is about two months old and still has the last of its spots;
these will finally disappear when it has its first moult in the autumn.

Play fight
Young stags practice their moves in preparation for the rutting season.

AUTUMN

The rut or mating season begins early in the autumn and lasts for approximately six weeks. It begins with the stags mingling among the hinds and calves. Eventually the largest and most powerful stags rush other male deer in the group as a show of superiority. Occasionally two big stags of similar size will battle for control of a group of hinds. They charge at one another with clashing antlers for a battle that can last up to half-an-hour. Eventually one stag will admit defeat and slink away but whilst the battle occurs it is likely that another stag will slip in and make off with the hinds. Throughout the rut the stags take to roaring – or 'belving' – out their challenges across the woods and combes. They try to rest during the day but have to rouse themselves continuously to round up hinds that wander, or drive off a young stag. By the end of December most of the stags have moved away to regroup in their own herds.

Stag in wallow
This splendid stag has been rolling in a mud pit (a wallow).

Opposite page: **Mingling**
This stag has rounded up several hinds in
preparation for the mating season.

Anyone home?
A stag and hinds explore a disused barn at Northmoor Hill.

A family affair
Another stag with hinds near Hindnam Lane.

A roaring stag during the autumn rut

Opposite page:
Feeling lonely
A solitary hind strays away from the herd for a while.

Belving

What a shock!
I was sitting in a tree during the rutting season when suddenly
this roaring stag appeared below me.

Roar
A lovely big stag at Draydon Rails.

Opposite page:
Kiss me quick
Getting affectionate during the mating season.

Black stag
The colouring of this particular stag was so dark, he was extremely noticeable.

Open wide
Another fine stag roaring at Warren Farm, near Simonsbath.

Opposite page:
Nature takes its course!

Resting
Taking a breather during the rutting season.